PHILLIP MARGULIES

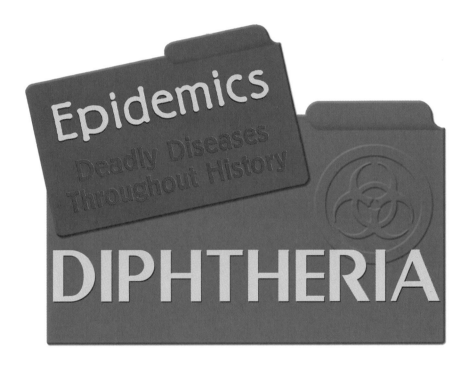

Epidemics
Deadly Diseases
Throughout History

DIPHTHERIA

The Rosen Publishing Group, Inc.
New York

Published in 2005 by The Rosen Publishing Group, Inc.
29 East 21st Street, New York, NY 10010

Library of Congress Cataloging-in-Publication Data

Margulies, Phillip, 1952–
Diphtheria/by Phillip Margulies.—1st ed.
    p. cm.—(Epidemics)
Includes bibliographical references and index.
ISBN 1-4042-0253-6 (lib. bdg.)
1. Diphtheria—History—Juvenile literature.
I. Title. II. Series.
RC138.1.M375 2005
616.9'313—dc22

                                        2004013395

Manufactured in the United States of America

On the cover: A plate culture of the diphtheria bacterium

CONTENTS

DIPHTHERIA STRIKES UNPROTECTED CHILDREN

PROTECT YOUR CHILD WITH TOXOID

TOXOID PREVENTS DIPHTHERIA

This 1930s Chicago Department of Health poster urges parents to inoculate their children with "toxoid," the diphtheria vaccine. Public health campaigns like this one have greatly reduced the death rates from diseases like diphtheria.

INTRODUCTION

Many of us think of the 1800s—the days of the horse and buggy, gaslights, and steam power—as a simpler time in the United States, when life was easier, quieter, and more peaceful than it is today. Americans did not worry about automobile accidents, ecological damage, or nuclear weapons. Most people lived on farms or in small towns. The pace of life was slower.

This nostalgic picture leaves a lot out, however, because people in the 1800s also had serious problems and worries that concern us far less today. One of their biggest worries was childhood disease. During the 1800s, children in Europe and the United States were in far greater danger of serious illness than they are now. Every year, epidemics of diseases such as scarlet fever, measles, mumps, and whooping cough swept through communities like the angel of death, carrying many children away forever.

One of the most feared killers of the time was diphtheria, a disease caused by a germ that usually found its way to the mouth, throat, and nose of an infected person, causing breathing difficulties, suffocation, heart failure, and paralysis. Though some adults did catch diphtheria, it was far more likely to attack young children. During a severe epidemic, it often killed more than one child in a family.

Doctors first named and clinically described diphtheria in the early 1800s. The peak years of the diphtheria epidemics in continental Europe, England, and the United States occurred between 1870 and 1920. Fear of diphtheria ran so high that newspapers often covered individual outbreaks of the disease. During this period, diphtheria epidemics occurred almost every year in the fall and winter in all the temperate regions of the earth. Throughout the 1920s, it struck, on average, about 150,000 people per year in the United States and killed about 15,000 of them. In 1921, there were 206,939 recorded cases of diphtheria in the United States alone. Before effective treatments were found, deaths from diphtheria were frequent.

The story of diphtheria is a tragic one for the millions of victims who lived before the second half of the twentieth century and the discovery of a treatment for disease. This discovery is one of modern medicine's greatest success stories. Scientists and doctors can point with pride to what they have achieved to combat diphtheria. The danger of this dreaded childhood enemy has been greatly reduced. Thanks especially to vaccines, diphtheria, once called "the strangling angel of children," has become a rarity in the developed world, and the fight against it has been carried to Africa, Asia, and Central America.

1

DIPHTHERIA: INFECTION, SYMPTOMS, AND TREATMENT

Diphtheria can take several different forms. It can be a relatively mild disease or a deadly one. It can infect people's skin or their airways, the body parts we use for breathing. In the cold and temperate climates of Europe and North America, diphtheria is best known as an illness of the nose and throat. Like the common cold and the flu, this form of diphtheria is what doctors call an upper respiratory infection. An upper respiratory disease is an illness that affects the body parts we use for breathing, especially the upper parts of that system that include the throat and nasal passages.

The most common symptoms of diphtheria are a sore throat, a low-grade fever, and the appearance of a "false membrane"—a slimy, leathery barrier—in the victim's throat. This membrane can make it hard for the victim to breathe. The resulting respiratory failure was a frequent cause of death in the days before effective preventions and treatments were found. Sometimes it still results in death in parts of the world that are not equipped to fight the disease.

How Diphtheria Is Contracted

Diphtheria is highly contagious. You can catch it from the cough or sneeze of someone who has it. In its early stages, diphtheria can seem like a cold, so those who are infected do not know it right away, and they can unknowingly infect others. In addition, some people are carriers of diphtheria—that is, they never come down with diphtheria's serious symptoms and never even know that they have diphtheria. Without realizing it, however, they can pass it on to others who get the more serious version of the disease. In countries where diphtheria vaccination is widespread, a relatively harmless version of the disease is common and infection usually goes unnoticed and poses no danger. The more dangerous strains of diphtheria are rare in these countries, so catching diphtheria is unlikely even for the unvaccinated. If someone who is unvaccinated against diphtheria travels to a part of the world where the disease is still prevalent, however, he or she is at risk.

Like most contagious diseases, diphtheria is caused by a germ that makes copies of itself once it gets inside its victim. The germ that causes diphtheria is a microscopic, rod-shaped bacterium scientists call *Corynebacterium diphtheriae (C. diphtheriae* for short). *C. diphtheriae* reproduces itself by splitting into two again and again until, quite quickly, there are billions of germs inside the infected person. When the person with diphtheria coughs or sneezes, copies of the germ exit the body and travel through the air in tiny droplets that another person can unknowingly breathe in.

As this picture illustrates, a sneeze can propel a great deal of material into the air, making it easy for another person to breathe in germs and spread respiratory diseases.

Bacteria (the plural of "bacterium") are very tiny, one-celled creatures that can be seen under a strong microscope. They are the oldest forms of life on earth.

Scientists do not know how many kinds of bacteria there are. Around 6,000 species of bacteria have been found so far, most of them as different from one another as a spider is different from a giraffe. There may be as many as a million different species of bacteria in existence. Most bacteria are harmless to human beings. In fact, there are more bacteria in a healthy person's mouth than there are people in the world. Some bacteria are essential to life on our planet, and many of them live in our bodies without our taking much if any notice of them. However, a handful of species of bacteria can be counted among humanity's deadliest enemies. *C. diphtheriae* is one of these.

Some close relatives of *C. diphtheriae* often infect animals, and *C. diphtheriae* itself can be grown on test animals. Ordinarily, however, it makes its home only in human beings and in only a few specific body parts. *C. diphtheriae* lives in the skin and the mucous membranes. Mucous membranes are the moist parts of our bodies that are sometimes exposed to the air, such as the lips, nasal passages, mouth, and throat. *C. diphtheriae* spreads from person to person through the mucus, skin cuts, bruises, and airborne droplets from the breath of those who have the disease.

As much as a week can go by between the time victims of diphtheria are infected with the illness and the first appearance of symptoms. Several more weeks

This electron micrograph shows the components of household dust: pollen, fungi, clothing and plant fibers, and skin flakes, which can harbor C. diphtheriae *and other bacteria.*

can pass before they know that they have anything more serious than a cold or flu. The symptom-free period and the relatively mild coldlike period are the times when those with diphtheria are most likely to spread the infection to others. As a rule, diphtheria is contagious for no more than four weeks. Some people infected with diphtheria never develop its symptoms and never realize they have the infection. For up to four weeks, these people can be carriers who, without knowing it, are responsible for spreading the illness to others.

The bacterium that causes diphtheria can also survive for up to six months in dust (dust contains small flakes of human skin) and in inanimate objects such as the clothing or bedding of people with diphtheria. People can then be infected by these dust particles and inanimate objects. While the idea of catching diphtheria from microscopic dust particles, clothing, or a doorknob is scary, it is a fairly uncommon occurrence. Most people catch diphtheria directly from an infected person.

The Symptoms of Diphtheria Infection

Most of the symptoms and deaths caused by *Corynebacterium diphtheriae* result from a toxin (poison) that the bacterium releases once it gets inside the human body. The more mild strains of the diphtheria bacterium do not release this poison, and the illness is much less severe as a result.

The symptoms that make diphtheria a killer are produced by the toxin-releasing strains of the bacterium. The poison first kills cells in the part of the victim's body where the bacteria have built up. The places this cell-killing bacterium picks to live often include the body parts we use for breathing, which is one reason why diphtheria can endanger human life. Later on, the poison may spread to other parts of the body, causing other kinds of damage.

The early symptoms of diphtheria are the same as those of many other upper respiratory diseases. Most people who have been infected will get a fever and chills. Almost all will get a sore throat. Some will become hoarse, and about half of those infected will feel swollen around the neck. Coughs, headaches, and nausea are also early symptoms of diphtheria, as they are of many other upper respiratory illnesses.

People who are infected by diphtheria through their skin tend to get painful, oozing, gray sores. In cold and temperate climates, it is more common to catch diphtheria through airborne droplets and to be infected in the nose and throat. People with this form of diphtheria may look pale, and the toxic bacteria will create bad breath. They will run a high fever and may have a rapid heartbeat.

One of the most frightening symptoms of diphtheria is the false membrane that appears in the victim's throat. The false membrane is thick and gray-brown in color. It may bleed if it is touched. It can choke a patient if it breaks and clogs the throat. Even if it remains in place, it can still cause choking if it grows large enough. For many years, doctors found themselves helpless to combat this membrane that put their young patients in a stranglehold. It was dangerous to leave it alone, yet often just as dangerous when the doctors tried to fight it, because surgically removing the membrane could cause choking or bleeding in the underlying tissue. The false membrane is still danger-ous when it occurs today in diphtheria sufferers, though doctors have developed better treatments for it, such as the use of a breathing tube until the membrane begins to shrink.

Other symptoms of diphtheria can also be painful, and some can be deadly. The infected parts of the body—often the throat and neck—usually become very swollen. At times, diph-theria has been called "bull-neck" because of the swelling it sometimes causes. People affected with diphtheria often find it difficult to speak as a result. Diphtheria can also lead to death by

In this 1942 photograph, a doctor changes a metal breathing tube in the throat of a patient suffering from inflammation caused by diphtheria.

heart failure. When the toxins released by the bacteria spread through the body, they can cause nerve and organ damage, including damage to the heart, kidneys, liver, and eyes. As many as 10 to 15 percent of people with diphtheria develop serious heart problems.

Who Gets Diphtheria?

In the days before a diphtheria vaccination was developed, children were far more likely to get diphtheria than were adults. Today, in countries like the United States, where almost all children are vaccinated against diphtheria, adults are actually more vulnerable to the illness than children. Because widespread vaccination against diphtheria has been under way in North America for more than half a century now, most of the adults who get the disease today were vaccinated against diphtheria when they were children. For this reason, these diphtheria cases among adults are something of a puzzle. Scientists think that the reason vaccinated adults may still catch diphtheria is that immunity from vaccinations eventually wears off.

Adults may also be at risk for getting diphtheria if, for some reason, their immune systems are weakened. The immune system is the body's protective defense against germs and viruses. The immune system can be weakened if it is put under regular stress. So, for example, alcoholics and drug users often develop weakened immunity and can more easily be infected by various diseases. The immune system can also be put under stress in crowded or unclean conditions, such as jails, tenements, and homeless shelters, where diphtheria infection is not uncommon. As we get older, our bodies get weaker, and the same is true of our immune systems. For this reason, elderly people run a greater risk of developing diphtheria as well as other infectious diseases.

Since diphtheria is contagious, everyone who has had contact with somebody who has diphtheria is considered to be at risk for developing the disease and should see a physician right away. Whenever doctors diagnose someone with diphtheria, they start testing the people with whom that patient has had contact to see if they have been infected with a dangerous strain of *C. diphtheriae*.

Treatment of Diphtheria

Because diphtheria does its damage through the toxin, or poison, that some strains of the bacterium *C. diphtheriae* release, the first line of treatment for diphtheria is an antitoxin. Antitoxins are chemicals that neutralize—or make harmless—poisons. Unfortunately, some people have allergic reactions to antitoxins. Before doctors give their patients the diphtheria antitoxin, therefore, they have to perform tests to see if it is safe for the patient and then decide how large a dose to give. They perform these tests and get the antitoxin to the patient as fast as possible, because the longer the antitoxin works on the patient the more time it has to eliminate the poisons. Usually, the doctors treating diphtheria also give patients antibiotics, which are drugs that kill bacteria.

Having diphtheria once does not always prevent someone from getting it again. So, as soon as diphtheria patients have recovered, doctors give them a treatment to boost their immunity to diphtheria. The treatment consists of the regular diphtheria vaccination that most children in North America and Europe get. Unlike most vaccinations, however, the diphtheria vaccination does not make people immune to infection of *C. diphtheriae*. Rather, the vaccination gives patients an immunity to the toxin released by *C. diphtheriae*. The vaccination is called the diphtheria toxoid, and its development has saved millions of lives worldwide.

2

HISTORIC OUTBREAKS OF DIPHTHERIA

The first human being to suffer from diphtheria may have been infected by a cow. Medical researchers believe this is true because a close relative of *C. diphtheriae*, the microbe that is the primary cause of diphtheria, is found in cows. Many diseases that afflict humans resemble illnesses that are found in farm animals. According to one theory, human beings caught most of these diseases when they first began to domesticate animals back in prehistoric times. So diphtheria may have first infected people around 3000 BC, when the inhabitants of Mesopotamia tamed the wild aurochs, whose descendants are modern cows.

The first ancient description of a disease that resembles diphtheria was recorded by the Greek physician Hippocrates in the fourth century BC. In

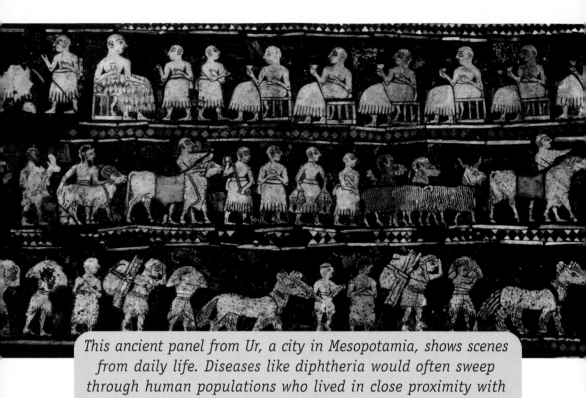

This ancient panel from Ur, a city in Mesopotamia, shows scenes from daily life. Diseases like diphtheria would often sweep through human populations who lived in close proximity with their livestock and each other.

the second century AD, during the time of the Roman Empire, a doctor named Aretaeus the Cappadocian described a condition very much like diphtheria. Some historians believe that diphtheria may also have existed in ancient Syria and Egypt.

Diphtheria in Early Modern Times

In 1576, Paris and several other European cities suffered from diphtheria epidemics. Although the disease had yet to be given a single, universal name, the symptoms described at the time by a physician named Guillaume de Baillou closely match those of diphtheria. In the sixteenth, seventeenth, and eighteenth centuries, epidemics of diphtheria appear to have occurred in Holland, Spain, Italy, and France, as well as in England. It can be hard for historians to be sure which of these epidemics were diphtheria, or how many people were affected, because at the time, the disease was lumped together with other respiratory infections. For example, both diphtheria and scarlet fever were called "throat distemper."

Descriptions of diphtheria in seventeenth-

This sixteenth-century portrait of Hippocrates shows him dissecting a cow's head. Hippocrates was one of the first to advocate a rational, scientific approach to medicine, and to describe a disease that closely resembles diphtheria.

century Spain, though, are more detailed and precise. It was known there as *el garatillo* ("the strangler"). In Italy and Sicily, diphtheria was called "the gullet disease." In 1735 to 1740, epidemics of diphtheria and scarlet fever spread throughout the New England colonies. Hundreds of people died, most of them children.

In 1826, the physician M. Bretonneau of Tours, France, presented the French Academy of Medicine with a paper describing a condition he called "la diphiherite." This term was derived from the Greek for "leather," and referred to the leathery false membrane that forms in the throats of diphtheria sufferers. Bretonneau's paper made a clear distinction between diphtheria and conditions like scarlet fever, and it also noted the sharp differences between the milder and more severe forms of diphtheria.

Diphtheria Becomes Endemic

It was during the middle of the 1800s that diphtheria became one of the most feared diseases of early childhood in Europe and North America. The outbreak that spread the disease across much of the Western world began in the middle of the century. In the winter of 1855 to 1856, 366 deaths from diphtheria occurred in the French city of Boulogne. Several of the deaths occurred among English visitors to the city. Some of the surviving visitors probably brought the disease home with them, because soon afterward cases began to be reported in southeast England. The disease soon spread throughout the entire country. By March 1858, diphtheria reached London, where it remained as an endemic disease. Scientists classify a disease as endemic when, at any given time, someone in a given area can be found who has the disease. In other words, if a disease never disappears completely from a certain area, it is considered endemic. Illnesses often become endemic when they reach large population centers. No matter how many people die from the disease or recover from it, the disease will always find someone new to infect.

The nineteenth century was the heyday of the British Empire, a worldwide empire so vast that it was said that the sun never set on it. English soldiers, administrators, and merchants traveled throughout the world, spreading their language, their ideals, their culture, and their germs. Perhaps for this reason, once diphtheria found its way to England from France, it soon traveled very quickly to every part of the world. Indeed, it reached the British colony of Australia in 1859, only one year after first being reported in London.

Diphtheria and the Industrial Revolution

The 1800s were an especially bad time for infectious diseases in the countries of the Northern Hemisphere.

Millions of people were prey not only to diphtheria, but also to a host of other diseases such as influenza (the flu), measles, mumps, scarlet fever, whooping cough, tuberculosis, rheumatic fever, typhoid fever, and syphilis. One reason the people of the 1800s suffered so greatly from these illnesses was that they were born too early to benefit from the great medical discoveries that occurred late in the century, when scientists discovered the germs that caused many of these diseases. Once the germs were identified and understood, scientists were able to develop treatments and methods of prevention.

Greater vulnerability to disease in the nineteenth century is also related to the great historical changes under way in the Western Hemisphere. During the 1800s, the economies of western Europe and the United States were transformed. Millions of former agricultural laborers were leaving the farms and finding a new kind of work in city factories, where they were paid to manufacture goods that were sold all over the world. The work of highly skilled craftsmen, who provided a relatively small number of handmade goods for those who could afford them, was replaced by the labor of men and women who operated machines that produced inexpensive goods in mass quantities. Historians call this great economic change the Industrial Revolution.

Eventually, the Industrial Revolution improved the lives of many people by making a wide range of useful household goods easily available at reasonable prices. Initially, however, it created much social dislocation, as people were uprooted from their rural homes, moved to overcrowded dirty cities, and began working in noisy and often dangerous factories. While industrialization made factory owners rich, it often brought grinding poverty to millions of their employees. The new factory workers worked very long hours to earn barely enough to live on. They and their families lived in filthy, overcrowded slums, eating a limited assortment of foods that was not enough to sustain good health.

This circa 1889 photo shows the interior of a tenement in New York City. Lack of ventilation and crowded conditions made tenements ideal breeding grounds for diseases like diphtheria.

Living and working conditions in the 1800s provided ideal breeding grounds for germs. In cities, factories, and tenement buildings, people were crowded together, increasing the number of daily contacts between them. As a result, germs had plenty of opportunities to spread by hand and through drinking water. Many people did not get enough vitamins or protein in their diets, so their general health was poor and their immune systems were weakened. Meanwhile, world-wide trade had expanded as never before, thus germs traveled quickly and far. While the new industrial workers suffered the most, epidemics among the poor often spread quickly to the rich, whose food was pre-pared by servants drawn from the working classes.

Diphtheria was simply a part of daily life for most of the nineteenth century. People had large families in those days, and it was quite common to lose one's young brother, sister, son, or daughter to a childhood illness. We can get an idea of the toll taken by diph-theria by noting some of the victims in the families of well-known historical figures. The American writer Mark Twain lost his son, Langdon, to diphtheria in 1872. In the same year, Jefferson Davis, who was pres-ident of the Confederacy (the union of rebellious Southern states) during the Civil War, lost his ten-year-old son, William, to diphtheria. U.S. president Dwight D. Eisenhower's brother, Paul, died of the dis-ease in early childhood. The mother of the British philosopher Bertrand Russell died of diphtheria as an adult, as did the mother of Eleanor Roosevelt, wife of U.S. president Franklin D. Roosevelt. Harry Truman, the president who took office after Roosevelt's death, barely survived a nearly fatal bout of the disease when he was a child. Diphtheria's deadly grasp even reached Europe's royal families: Queen Victoria's daughter, Alice, died of diphtheria as an adult in an outbreak that spread throughout the palace.

This 1860 photo of England's Princess Alice was taken when she was about seventeen years old. She died of diphtheria at age thirty-five, probably caught from family members she was nursing through the illness.

For every victim among the wealthy and prominent, diphtheria claimed the lives of many more ordinary citizens. For a time during the late nineteenth century, diphtheria was the leading cause of death among children. In 1888, London's Metropolitan Asylums Board hospitals, which served the poor, began to accept diphtheria cases. Because doctors did not yet have any effective treatments for diphtheria, the hospitals did not so much hope to treat or cure the disease as to halt its spread by isolating the patients and removing them from the general population. It was hoped that the disease would die with them.

Although the diphtheria epidemic was at its worst in the United States in the late nineteenth century, reliable medical statistics were not kept until the early part of the twentieth century, when the disease was on the wane. Even then, however, the incidence of diphtheria infection was very high. In the 1920s, for example, there were about 150,000 diphtheria cases and 15,000 diphtheria-related deaths reported each year.

Diphtheria in Decline

By the beginning of the twentieth century, scientists had found the cause of diphtheria and developed a diphtheria antitoxin—a treatment that neutralized the poison released by the bacterium *C. diphtheriae*. Later, during the 1920s, scientists developed a treatment to immunize people in advance against the poison. Immunization involves exposing someone to a mild form of the diphtheria toxin so that his or her immune system will fight the toxin. In so doing, the immune system will develop antibodies (proteins that fight toxins) that

This 1946 photo shows mothers in London bringing their children to receive diphtheria vaccinations. The disruptions and stresses of World War II had led to a rise in diphtheria rates across Europe, but since then, immunization and improved hygiene have made the disease rare in most Western countries.

will protect the body against more severe forms of the disease (see chapter 4).

It took many years before the diphtheria immunization treatment could be delivered to most American children. In the meantime, however, public sanitation and overall public health improved, leading to fewer diphtheria cases as well as fewer deaths. In the United States, diphtheria cases had fallen to 19,000 by 1945—about one-seventh of the infection rate in the 1920s. This decline was matched by similar declines in other temperate regions, such as Europe, where diphtheria had caused so much suffering. In the late 1940s, doctors in the United States and Europe began to make immunization against diphtheria an important element of routine medical exams. Soon afterward, diphtheria was on its way to becoming a rare disease.

Since the middle of the twentieth century, diphtheria outbreaks have occurred in the West mainly during times of social disorder when public systems break down, such as in wartime. A shortage of food, dirty water, stress, lack of good medical care, and overcrowding can all reduce the general health of a population and make disease spread. During World War II (1939–1945), there were diphtheria outbreaks in many European countries. In 1943 alone, there were around a million cases of diphtheria across Europe, resulting in almost 50,000 deaths. Following the collapse of the Soviet Union in 1991, and the resulting breakdown of social services in some of the former Soviet republics, 50,000 cases of diphtheria were reported.

While these occasional outbreaks of diphtheria are tragic, it is a tribute to the success of modern medicine and public health that they are now the exception, not the rule.

3

THE ROAD TO A CURE

In the 1870s, diphtheria was a riddle. So were most infectious diseases. Over a relatively short period of time around the end of the nineteenth century, medical scientists solved this riddle, finding the causes and developing treatments for diphtheria and many other diseases that had plagued humanity throughout history. Their achievements occurred during one of the most exciting times in the history of medicine. During this time, a handful of researchers in France, Germany, England, and the United States, led by Louis Pasteur and Robert Koch, developed the germ theory of disease. The medical world's understanding of infectious diseases and its ability to fight them was about to take a great leap forward.

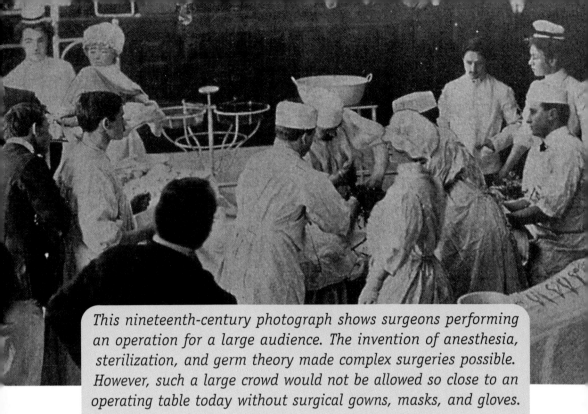

This nineteenth-century photograph shows surgeons performing an operation for a large audience. The invention of anesthesia, sterilization, and germ theory made complex surgeries possible. However, such a large crowd would not be allowed so close to an operating table today without surgical gowns, masks, and gloves.

The Beginning of the Germ Theory

The development and testing of the germ theory is a surprisingly recent event in the history of science, especially considering that medicine has been practiced for many thousands of years. By the early 1800s, many scientists had become aware of the existence of tiny living things, which they saw through microscopes. Most doctors, however, remained unaware of them and scoffed at the idea that they could possibly be the cause of disease. Bad air, rather than unsanitary conditions, was thought to be the cause of many illnesses. Hospitals were designed to offer plenty of ventilation but were not especially clean. For example, surgeons did not even change into clean clothing or wash their hands and their instruments before they operated on their patients. These unsanitary practices resulted in infections among patients, many of which were fatal.

To be fair to the doctors of the time, it should be noted that the microscopes of the early 1800s were not powerful enough to make most disease-causing germs visible. Still, there was other evidence of the existence of germs, which most doctors ignored. For example, one of the most common causes of death in women was a disease

Ignaz Semmelweiss (above) *was one of the first to understand the role of hygiene in preventing disease. Unfortunately, he was ignored or ridiculed for his ideas, and died largely unappreciated for his efforts.*

called childbed fever, an illness that often struck women after they gave birth—especially if they gave birth in hospitals where they were attended by medical students. In the 1850s, a Hungarian physician named

Fourth century BC
Greek physician Hippocrates provides the first clinical description of diphtheria.

1858
Diphtheria becomes endemic in London after arriving from France. It reaches the British colony of Australia by 1859.

1894
A diphtheria antitoxin is developed and produced by Shibasaburo Kitasato and Emil von Behring.

1576
Paris and other European cities suffer from diphtheria outbreaks.

1884
The bacterium that causes diphtheria is discovered by Edwin Klebs and Friedrich Loeffler.

1900s
Diphtheria is one of the leading causes of death in infants and children in the United States.

Ignaz Semmelweiss noticed that the death rates among women with the fever were extra high in the teaching hospitals, where medical students went straight from dissecting corpses to delivering children in the maternity ward. Semmelweiss ordered the doctors under his supervision to wash their hands in chlorinated lyme before they entered the maternity ward. The death rate immediately dropped.

As obvious as they seem today, Semmelweiss's ideas were very controversial at the time and made him the

1920s
About 150,000 cases of diphtheria are reported in the United States, with 15,000 deaths.

Late 1940s
Following the introduction of universal diphtheria immunization, diphtheria cases fall to 19,000 in the United States.

1959–1980
Seven outbreaks of fifteen or more cases of diphtheria occur in the United States. No outbreaks of fifteen or more cases occur after 1980.

1943
Almost a million people are infected with diphtheria in war-torn Europe, and 50,000 die.

1993
Fifty thousand cases of diphtheria are reported in some of the former Soviet republics following the collapse of the Soviet Union.

enemy of the most respected surgeons of the day. By the 1870s, though, ideas similar to those of Semmelweiss were also being advanced by the Scottish surgeon Joseph Lister. He was eventually able to gain wide acceptance for them.

Meanwhile, a French chemist named Louis Pasteur and a German doctor named Robert Koch, working separately, conducted the research that established the basics of germ theory. In 1857, Pasteur proved that invisible microbes, present in the air, were what made food go bad. Working on the theory that invisible microorganisms might also be responsible for disease, Pasteur was able to prevent the spread of diseases affecting silkworms and sheep. Pasteur went on to invent the technique named after him—pasteurization—that is used to remove harmful organisms from milk and make it safe to drink. In addition, he developed the first vaccines for anthrax, chicken cholera, and rabies.

While Pasteur was trying to prove the existence of invisible organisms based on their visible effects on plants and animals, Robert Koch was inventing the modern science of bacteriology, the study of the microscopic organisms called bacteria. Koch suspected that these tiny creatures could be a major cause of disease. His research took advantage of recent improvements in microscopes that had made them powerful enough to see bacteria. Koch began by collecting bacteria from sick animals. He isolated the bacteria, growing them in containers so that each container contained only one type of bacteria. He then put the bacteria into the bodies of healthy animals. The healthy animals became sick with the same disease found in the animal that had originally provided the bacteria. Koch's work established many basic principles of bacteriology and disease that we take for granted today. Most important, it proved that certain types of germs cause certain types of disease.

Bacteriology quickly became an exciting new field of medical research. Doctors in France, Germany, England, and the United States went to work seeking the various kinds of bacteria that lay behind many of the world's most prevalent and deadly diseases.

Solving the Puzzle of Diphtheria

By the 1880s, the laboratories of Louis Pasteur in France and Robert Koch in Germany were world famous, and both Pasteur and Koch were assisted by young microbiologists eager to learn the new science and solve the riddles of infectious disease. Pasteur and Koch worked at a time of bitter rivalry between France and Germany—a rivalry that would eventually erupt into a world war—but the competition was useful in this instance. The two laboratories raced against each other to be the first to unlock the secrets of diphtheria, and children in many countries benefited from the results.

In 1883, Edwin Klebs, a professor at the University of Zurich in Switzerland, described a bacterium that he believed was the cause of diphtheria, although he was unable to prove it. A year later, Friederich Loeffler, a bacteriologist working under the supervision of Robert

Koch, proved that Klebs had been right. The bacterium, now commonly known as *C. diphtheriae*, is also called the Klebs-Loeffler bacillus, in honor of its discoverers. A bacillus is the name given to any rod-shaped bacterium. When he was experimenting on guinea pigs, Loeffler noticed that the test animals suffered diphtheria symptoms in parts of their bodies where no Klebs-Loeffler bacilli could be found. Yet other experiments had proved that the Klebs-Loeffler bacilli were the cause of the disease. So how did the bacteria cause damage in a part of the body so far from where they were growing? In a research paper, Loeffler suggested that the answer might be that the bacteria produced a toxin that traveled to other parts of the body. He admitted, however, that he had been unable to find this toxin.

The next steps in understanding diphtheria were taken at the Pasteur Institute in France by Louis Pasteur's assistants, Emile Roux and Alexandre Yersin. After three years of difficult laboratory research, Roux and Yersin proved that Loeffler's guess—that the bacillus produced a toxin—was correct. First, Roux and Yersin grew large colonies of toxin-releasing Klebs-Loeffler bacilli. Then they invented filters that strained out the microscopic bacteria and let through a bacteria-free liquid. This liquid alone caused the symptoms of diphtheria in

French physician and bacteriologist Emile Roux prepares his serum against diphtheria in this 1894 engraving. A pupil and colleague of Louis Pasteur's, Roux proved in 1888 that the diphtheria bacillus produces a toxin. This discovery eventually led to the creation of an antitoxin and effective treatments for the disease.

laboratory animals. The toxin that they discovered in the liquid was incredibly dangerous and potent. Roux estimated that one ounce of it would be enough to kill 600,000 guinea pigs or 75,000 large dogs. Their work pointed the way for other scientists to develop effective treatments of and preventive approaches to diphtheria.

Back in Koch's laboratory, two other scientists, Emil von Behring and Shibasaburo Kitasato continued the quest to cure diphtheria. After many experiments in which they gave various chemical compounds to animals they had infected with diphtheria, they found that under some circumstances, animals produced a

Emil von Behring (right) *is seen here in his lab with an assistant and several guinea pigs. For his work on diphtheria and tetanus immunizations, Behring won the 1901 Nobel Prize in Physiology or Medicine.*

substance that neutralized the effects of the diphtheria toxin. They called the substance an "antitoxin," and they proved that the antitoxin taken from the body of one animal could cure another animal's diphtheria. To work well, the antitoxin had to be administered in the early stages of diphtheria.

The discovery of an antitoxin for diphtheria made headlines all over the world. In 1894, Behring began to manufacture the antitoxin. That same year, the New York City Health Department began using it on patients with diphtheria. From that point on, diphtheria was in retreat throughout most of the developed world.

4

FROM CURE TO PREVENTION

By discovering the diphtheria antitoxin, Behring and Kitasato took medicine a giant step forward in the treatment of a terrible disease. Problems remained, however, and diphtheria continued to be a major killer. For one thing, to be fully effective, the antitoxin had to be given to patients very early in the course of the disease. Many patients with diphtheria received the antitoxin too late to be of any use. Another problem was the antitoxin itself. It was derived from the bloodstream of horses, and some patients had powerful allergic reactions to products produced from the horses' bodies. While death rates from diphtheria declined after the antitoxin was introduced, infections continued and deaths still occurred. Scientists began to search for a substance that would protect people from getting diphtheria in the first place rather than working on a cure for infection.

Boosting Diphtheria Immunity

Even before the germ theory of disease was developed, doctors knew that people who had gotten certain diseases once seemed to be protected from getting them again. This effect is called immunity. Doctors had even discovered, by trial and error, that scratching people's skin with powder taken from the sores of someone stricken with a relatively mild disease called cowpox would prevent them from catching a much more serious, often deadly disease called smallpox. They called this treatment vaccination. But doctors did not yet really understand how vaccination worked.

Even after the development of germ theory, scientists had a lot to learn about the process of immunity. All they really knew, by the turn of the century, was that the body had defenses against alien invaders. When an invading germ made someone sick, a sort of battle went on in his or her body. People could lose the battle, in which case they eventually died of the disease. If, however, they won the battle, they were often much more ready for a similar battle the next

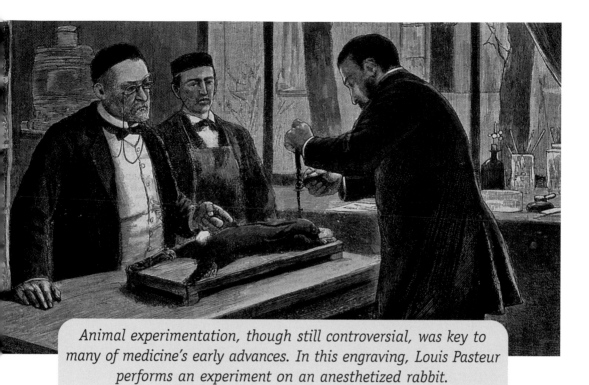

Animal experimentation, though still controversial, was key to many of medicine's early advances. In this engraving, Louis Pasteur performs an experiment on an anesthetized rabbit.

time the invader came. It was as if the body had learned something during the course of the first battle—a new way of fighting or a secret weapon— that made it better at fighting that particular enemy the next time it appeared. Today, after a great deal of additional research, the complex processes of immunity are well understood. We call the immune system's weapons against specific invaders antibodies, and we call the invaders that cause the defensive response antigens.

In the late 1800s, scientists began to look for ways to stimulate this mysterious response without making people ill. Louis Pasteur had the first success in this area. In 1885, he developed a vaccine that prevented people from getting rabies, the fatal disease people contracted from the bites of infected animals. Researchers at Pasteur's institute began to methodically look for ways to create similar vaccines for other diseases.

The basic idea behind most vaccines is to find an antigen—the substance that is known to cause both a disease and an immune response to the disease—and then to weaken it. Once weakened, the antigen would be put into a patient's bloodstream, stimulating his or her immune response without actually causing infection or full-blown disease. Though it sounds like a simple process, creating a vaccine can take many years. Twenty years after discovering the virus that causes AIDS, scientists have still not been able to invent a vaccine against it, despite the dedicated work of thousands of researchers and the investment of millions of dollars in the effort.

The Diphtheria Toxoid

In 1909, an American bacteriologist named Theobold Smith had a novel and daring idea. It was known that people who were exposed to the diphtheria toxin developed an immunity to it. How this immunity worked, no one knew for sure. Why not give children the toxin and the antitoxin at the same time, Smith asked. Children would then develop immunity without coming down with the symptoms of diphtheria, Smith reasoned, and they would not be in danger of getting the disease again. Smith's treatment was called the toxin-antitoxin complex, or TAT.

Starting around 1910, TAT began to be used to provide immunity against diphtheria. It never became widely used, however, because it had drawbacks. Some people reacted badly to the toxin in the mixture, despite the presence of the antitoxin. Others were allergic to the antitoxin itself. As bad as diphtheria was, the risks of TAT were too high to give it to children who might not ever even become infected with diphtheria.

At last, in 1924, Gaston Ramon, a French scientist working at the Pasteur Institute, developed a much safer vaccine against the diphtheria toxin. By treating the toxin with formaldehyde, Ramon rendered it harmless. The treated toxin, called diphtheria toxoid, could no longer cause damage to the human body. Though it was now harmless, the toxoid was still recognized by the human body as a foreign invader, so it caused an immune response. The body's immune system developed antibodies, which are specially designed to attack and neutralize the toxin. These antibodies remained in the body and provided protection against the future invasion of harmful diphtheria toxins. Ramon's toxoid provided long-term

Nome, Alaska, is a very cold place, located just two degrees latitude below the Arctic Circle. A blizzard was brewing in the winter of 1925, when the local doctor, Curtis Welch, recognized the signs of a serious diphtheria outbreak. Several of his patients had already died. The sickness was spreading. Welch knew that the best chance he had to save his patients was to give them the diphtheria antitoxin. Unfortunately, none was locally available. Dr. Welch sent out an urgent message over the radio, saying the town had to have the diphtheria antitoxin in order to fight a major outbreak of the disease.

The situation would have been considered an emergency wherever it happened, but the medical authorities trying to get the lifesaving antitoxin from Anchorage to Nome confronted some unique problems. The antitoxin could not be brought by boat, because pack ice had developed in the Nome harbor and other waterways. The nearest railroad to Nome was nearly 700 miles (1,126.5 kilometers) away. The blizzard made bringing the antitoxin in by airplane impossible. Under those circumstances, the best way to get the antitoxin from the railhead to Nome would be by dogsled relay. After a train brought the antitoxin from Anchorage to the town of Nenona, a series of dogsled teams would race to carry the antitoxin the rest of the way.

Dogsled drivers and their teams of dogs raced by night in subfreezing temperatures and high winds to deliver the antitoxin. Gunnar Kaasen and a team of Siberian huskies led by the lead dog, Balto, traveled the last 53 miles (85 km) in temperatures of -63° Fahrenheit (-51° Celsius) and 70 mile-per-hour (113 km/h) winds. Balto found his way

Gunnar Kaasen poses with Balto (left) *and the statue commemorating their heroic journey that was installed in Central Park, New York City, in 1925.*

through the storm to the town, the antitoxin was delivered, and lives were saved. In honor of his heroic effort, a statue of Balto was placed in New York City's Central Park.

To commemorate this lifesaving journey, a world-famous dogsled race is held on the first Saturday in March every year in Alaska. It is called the Iditarod, after the name of the trail that runs from the port of Seward to the city of Nome.

immunity to diphtheria, especially when given repeatedly over a period of years. It formed the basis for the immunization program that has turned diphtheria into a rare disease in the countries where it was once a common but terrifying fact of life.

Further Pieces of the Puzzle

The discovery of the basic facts about diphtheria, and the development of a treatment and prevention for it, were triumphs of the new science of microbiology. Yet there were still many unsolved problems related to diphtheria. The biggest of all was the question of why the diphtheria bacterium was sometimes deadly and at other times provoked only a relatively mild illness.

In 1951, V. J. Freeman, a scientist at the University of Wisconsin, made a remarkable discovery that solved a large part of this puzzle. By the time that Freeman was performing his research, scientists had learned that, in addition to bacteria, there are also even smaller infectious germs called viruses. Viruses cause infectious diseases like the common cold, the flu, and measles. They are so small that they cannot be seen under even the most powerful light microscopes that Robert Koch and his assistants used to explore the hidden world of bacteria. It was not until the 1930s, when the electron microscope was invented, that scientists got their first look at a virus. All living things can be infected by viruses. Plants get them, animals get them—even bacteria get them. Ironically, bacteria, which are the cause of so much sickness in animals and human beings, can get sick themselves. Viruses infect bacteria. Sometimes viruses kill the bacteria they

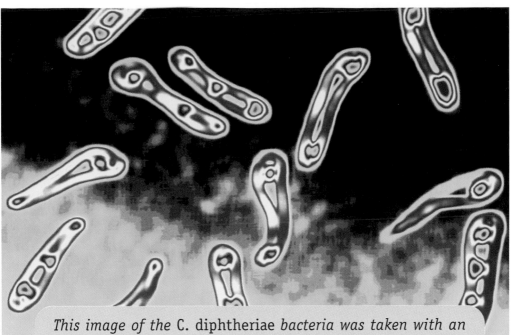

This image of the C. diphtheriae *bacteria was taken with an electron microscope. Regular microscopes cannot distinguish objects that are smaller than 0.275 micrometers. Electron microscopes, on the other hand, can magnify objects up to one million times, making it possible to study bacteria and viruses closely.*

infect. At other times, they alter the behavior of the bacteria. Viruses that specialize in infecting bacteria are called phages. Freeman, studying *C. diphtheriae*, found that it was sometimes infected by a phage. The strains of *C. diphtheriae* that released deadly toxins had all been infected by a phage. The relatively harmless strains of diphtheria had not been infected by a phage. A phage that infects *C. diphtheriae* causes it to release the toxin, turning it from a mild source of infection into a deadly killer.

5

DIPHTHERIA YESTERDAY AND TODAY

The toxin-producing form of respiratory diphtheria, once a major childhood killer, has become a rare disease today. This did not happen overnight, though diphtheria infection declined soon after the diphtheria toxoid was introduced. It did not even happen within a few years of the discoveries that led to the development of an effective diphtheria vaccine. Rather, the near-disappearance of diphtheria occurred over the course of decades.

Why did it take so long to get rid of the disease, when all of the major discoveries that helped to combat it were made by 1924? The main reason is that many years passed before everyone received a vaccination that used the diphtheria toxoid. Communities that regarded diphtheria as a major problem—big cities like New York and London—tried to immunize as many children as possible right away. Cases of diphtheria declined in those places, but they also declined in other places where vaccination had not been widely practiced. No one can say for sure why diphtheria cases declined even where people were not vaccinated. Like many other diseases, diphtheria comes and goes even without public health measures to treat it. It may also be that by the late 1920s, better sanitation, reduced overcrowding, and improved diet had led to reduced rates of diphtheria without the help of the vaccine.

In this 1925 photo, Dr. Bela Schick, at right, administers a test he created to detect immunity to diphtheria. It is still in use today.

The spotty use of vaccinations left many people vulnerable to diphtheria, however. Outbreaks occurred in Germany and in England in the late 1930s. Major diphtheria epidemics tend to occur in unsanitary and overcrowded conditions, such as in many parts of

Londoners gather at a fruit stand amid the rubble of bombed buildings during World War II. Lack of access to adequate, nutritious food can encourage diseases such as diphtheria.

Europe during and immediately after World War II. Universal diphtheria vaccination in advanced industrial countries did not begin until the late 1940s. Since that time, however, outbreaks of diphtheria have been extremely rare.

The Debate Surrounding Vaccination

Vaccination is a medical procedure that is usually performed on healthy children. Over the years, vaccinations for various infectious diseases have saved millions of lives, but they have also sometimes made some children sick. On very rare occasions, vaccinations have even killed those who received them. For this reason, ever since vaccinations were first introduced, some people have been strongly opposed to them.

Those in favor of vaccinations point to the dramatic decline of infectious diseases that has occurred in the places where vaccinations have been introduced. Those opposed to vaccinations say this decline has occurred for other reasons, such as improved sanitation, better nutrition, and less overcrowding. Vaccinations, they say, do not deserve the credit.

The debate is complicated because it is true that vaccinations are not the only reason for the decline of infectious diseases. Clean water, good housing, and sufficient and varied food supply are certainly crucial to good health and go a long way toward combating disease. Conversely, in the poorest countries of the world today, lack of access to these things is probably the most important cause of disease. Even in poor countries, however, vaccination has helped reduce outbreaks of diseases that used to cause millions of deaths. For example, vaccination has completely rid the world of smallpox. The virus that causes smallpox is extinct, and people no longer need to be vaccinated against it. Using similar methods, doctors would like to eradicate other deadly diseases as well.

Can Diphtheria Be Eradicated?

Could diphtheria, like smallpox, be made extinct? One day, perhaps it may, but probably not anytime soon. That is because, unlike the smallpox vaccine, the diphtheria toxoid does not really stop the spread of diphtheria. It merely protects people against the toxin that some forms of *C. diphtheriae* produce when they get inside the human body. To eradicate diphtheria, science would have to develop a vaccine against the bacterium itself, or at least against the toxic strain of the bacterium. Then doctors would have to vaccinate almost everybody in the world against diphtheria.

This is unlikely to happen soon, because diphtheria is not a major killer in the tropical countries where it is still widespread. In those countries, it usually takes the form of a mild skin infection, which goes away in a few weeks. For a long time to come, vaccination programs in tropical countries will concentrate on the diseases that are major killers, rather than diphtheria. So, for the foreseeable future, *C. diphtheriae* will continue to exist, and children in the temperate regions of the world will have to be vaccinated against its dangerous and sometimes deadly toxin.

GLOSSARY

antibiotics A class of drugs that kills bacteria.

bacterium A member of a class of single-celled microorganisms, some of which cause infections and disease in animals and humans. The plural of "bacterium" is "bacteria."

Corynebacterium diphtheriae The scientific name of the bacterium that causes the disease diphtheria. Also called the Klebs-Loeffler bacillus, named after the scientists who first described it and suggested its link to diphtheria.

diphtheria A serious infectious disease that produces a toxin (poison) and an inflammation in the lining of the throat, nose, trachea, and other body parts. A common symptom is a false membrane in the throat, which can obstruct breathing.

endemic Relating to a disease that is constantly present to a greater or lesser degree in people living in a particular location.

epidemic An outbreak of a contagious disease that spreads rapidly and widely.

germ theory The theory that particular microorganisms cause particular diseases.

immunity Protection against a disease.

immunization A medical procedure that provides protection against disease.

phage A virus that specializes in infecting bacteria.

toxin A poisonous substance.

toxoid A toxin (poison) stripped of its toxicity and then injected into the bloodstream to provoke an immune system response that will protect the body from actual toxins.

vaccine A preparation of weakened or killed microorganisms or proteins, administered for the prevention or treatment of infectious diseases.

virus A microorganism smaller than a bacteria that cannot grow or reproduce unless it is residing in living cells. Some scientists question whether a virus can be considered alive, since it cannot perform the basic functions of life on its own.

FOR MORE INFORMATION

In the United States

Centers for Disease Control and Prevention (CDC)
National Center for Infectious Diseases (NCID)
1600 Clifton Road
Atlanta, GA 30333
(404) 639-3311 or (800) 311-3435
Web site: http://www.cdc.gov/ncidod

National Institutes of Health (NIH)
9000 Rockville Pike
Bethesda, Maryland 20892
(301) 496-4000
Web site: http://www.nih.gov/about/contact.htm

National Network for Immunization Information
301 University Boulevard
CH 2.218
Galveston, TX 77555
(409) 772-0199
Web site: http://www.immunizationinfo.org

World Health Organization (WHO)
525 23rd Street, NW
Washington, DC 20037
(202) 974-3000
Web site: http://www.who.int/en

In Canada
Health Canada
A.L. 0900C2
Ottawa, Ontario K1A 0K9
(613) 957-2991 or (800) 267-1245
Web site: http://www.hc-sc.gc.ca/english

Web Sites
Due to the changing nature of Internet links, the Rosen Publishing Group, Inc., has developed an online list of Web sites related to the subject of this book. This site is updated regularly. Please use this link to access the list:

http://www.rosenlinks.com/epid/dipt

FOR FURTHER READING

Brunelle, Lynn, and Marc Gave, eds. *Viruses*.
Milwaukee, WI: Gareth Stevens, 2003.

De Kruif, Paul, and F. Gonzales-Cruissi. *Microbe Hunters*. New York: Harvest Books, 2002.

Hyde, Margaret O., and Elizabeth H. Forsyth, MD. *Vaccinations: From Smallpox to Cancer*. New York: Franklin Watts, 2000.

Jakab, E. A. M. *Louis Pasteur: Hunting Killer Germs*. New York: McGraw Hill/Contemporary Books, 2000.

Marsh, Carole. *The Official Guide to Germs*. Peachtree City, GA: Gallopade International, 2003.

Miller, Debbie S. *The Great Serum Race: Blazing the Iditarod Trail*. New York: Walker & Co., 2002.

Salisbury, Gay. *The Cruelest Miles: The Heroic Story of Dogs and Men in a Race Against an Epidemic*. New York: W. W. Norton & Company, 2003.

BIBLIOGRAPHY

Demirci, Cem S., MD, and Walid Abuhammour, MD. "Diphtheria." EMedicine.com. July 2002. Retrieved March 2004 (http://www.emedicine.com/ped/topic596.htm).

Desalle, Rob, ed. *Epidemic! The World of Infectious Disease*. New York: New Press, 1999.

Diamond, Jared. *Guns, Germs, and Steel: The Fates of Human Societies*. New York: W. W. Norton & Company, 1999.

"Edwin Klebs, Medicine, Biographies." AllRefer.com. 2003. Retrieved March 2004 (http://reference.allrefer.com/encyclopedia/K/Klebs-Ed.html).

"Emil von Behring—Biography." Nobel eMuseum. 2004. Retrieved March 2004 (http://www.nobel.se/medicine/laureates/1901/behring-bio.html).

Hardy, Anne. *The Epidemic Streets: Infectious Diseases and the Rise of Preventive Medicine, 1856–1900*. New York: Oxford University Press, 1993.

Karlen, Arno. *Man and Microbes: Disease and Plagues in History and Modern Times*. New York: Simon & Schuster, 1996.

Nuland, Sherwin B. *The Doctors' Plague: Germs, Childbed Fever, and the Strange Story of Ignac Semmelweis*. New York: W. W. Norton & Company, 2003.

"Pioneers in Medical Laboratory Science." Hoslink. Retrieved March 2004 (http://www. hoslink. com/PIONEERS.HTM).

Robbins, Louis. *Louis Pasteur and the Hidden World of Microbes*. New York: Oxford University Press, 2001.

Todar, Kenneth. "Corynebacterium diphtheriae." Bacteriology at UW-Madison, 2002. Retrieved March 2004 (http://www.bact.wisc.edu/Bact330/lecturediphth).

Ziporyn, Terra. *Disease in the Popular American Press: The Case of Diphtheria, Typhoid Fever, and Syphilis, 1870–1920*. Westport, CT: Greenwood Publishing Group, 1988.

INDEX

CREDITS

About the Author

Phillip Margulies is a freelance writer living in New York City.

Photo Credits